GOD'S
ANSWER
to the question of
EVIL

STEVE KERN

Foreword by Tom Eliff

For more information contact, Kern Enterprises,
2713 N. Sterling Ave., Oklahoma City. Ok. 73127
(405) 942-3504

All scripture references are from the New American
Standard Bible, translated by the Lockman
Foundation.

ISBN: 978-0-9798667-4-6

CONTENTS

FOREWORD

While few people deny the presence of evil, most are either ignorant, or at best unclear as to its source. So where did evil originate? How is evil sustained? And is there any possibility of triumph over evil? Steve Kern's book, God's Answer to the Question of Evil, is an excellent, accurate and thought-provoking primer on the subject of evil. Unlike many who treat the subject of evil on a merely philosophical level but leaves its readers hanging, Kern takes his readers on a journey with a bright conclusion. Kern reminds us that we can each personally triumph over evil and its impact on our lives...both now and forever.

Tom Elliff

INTRODUCTION

Evil, what is it, and where does it come from? These are questions that have troubled the minds of theologians and philosophers for millennia. Many people over the centuries have given up on their faith in God because of the hurt they have incurred due to evil done to them or their loved ones. Many Jews became atheists because of Hitler's holocaust. The existence of evil suggests a contradiction to some that if God the Creator is good, then how can a good God allow evil to exist in His creation?

I ran into this argument about evil more than once in my college days. As I struggled with finding the answer to this attack on my faith, I knew enough to not question the existence of God. What I needed was an answer to give in order to be faithful to 1 Peter 3:15 that encourages us to, "…always being ready to make a defense to everyone who ask you to give an account for the hope that is in you…" I found the answer to this apparent contradiction that has been in God's word from the very beginning of time. This book will give a step by step answer to the question of evil following the revelation God has given to us in the first three chapters of Genesis.

MAN'S EXPLANATIONS
OF EVIL

There is so much pain and suffering in the world starting with Cain killing his brother Abel, and then Lamech killing "a boy for striking me" in Genesis 4:23. Since then there have been wars, mass murders, slavery, rapes and carnage of every kind, human sacrifice, sexual perversion, diseases, plagues, natural disasters, genocide, theft, embezzlement, tyrannical kings and dictators, the list goes on and on. Yes, evil is a part of the human existence in this fallen world. We have all been impacted by it in one way or another as victims or culprits.

Down through history man has tried to explain why evil exists. The range of explanations have gone from evil spirits, to good gods verses bad gods, good karma and bad karma, demons, Satan, yin and yang, some people are born bad and some people are born good, and there are other explanations but you get the picture.

In western philosophy the explanations have ranged from God is weak and cannot control evil to the deist idea that God is disinterested and no longer involved in what goes on in His creation. And then, there is the atheistic explanation that because evil exists there can be no God at all. They answer if a good God exists there would be no evil because He would be incapable of evil or allowing it to exist in His good creation.

The interesting thing about doing away with God altogether is that the logical conclusion to the absence of God leaves us with no distinction between good or evil. Nothing can be said to be good and nothing can be said to be evil because there is no standard to make a distinction between the two. Evil becomes a matter of human determination without an ultimate authority.

This creates a problem for atheists. They have to deal with the fact that their worldview does away with good and evil all together. There is no good and there is no evil. It all becomes a matter of one's opinion as to what should be defined as good or evil, but these are just individual opinions with no absolute authority to justify the opinions, except in the mind of the individual holding the opinions. It's called relativism. This relativism leads to a dangerous conclusion that whoever has the power makes the rules. That is why atheism always leads to tyrannical, authoritarian, dictatorial governments.

There is a problem with this atheist point of view. We know evil does exist. The human experience has taught us that there are some things that are considered good and some things that are considered evil by every culture in the human race. Every society considers murder to be wrong. Freedom is held to be good. Every human wants to have dignity. There are "laws of nature and nature's God" that are considered to be universal in scope. The concept of human conscience and the human emotion of guilt suggest there is the reality of right and wrong. Yes, some things are good and some things are evil. Good and evil do exist.

C.S. Lewis was a well known Christian writer and apologist in the last century. He became convinced that his atheism could not be supported by the argument that

God could not exist because of the existence of evil. It occurred to him that without the existence of absolute good then evil would not exist. He could not deny that absolute good exists in human experience and in order for that good to be absolute it had to be an expression of a higher authority than man. That higher authority has to be God. In time, Lewis became a Christian by coming to the conclusion that the God of the Bible is the true source of absolute good.

One of the great apologetic arguments for the existence of God is referred to as the Moral Argument. It is based on the reality of the existence of good and evil. As C. S. Lewis came to realize, like so many others coming out of atheism, there is a Moral Absolute. According to the law of cause and effect, in order for morality to exist, there has to be a cause that can explain the effect we call morals. Morals are not self determined, they have to be an expression of a higher authority that causes all of humanity to be accountable to them. That higher authority has to be God.

So, logic teaches us that there has to be a morally good God in order for evil to exist. The questions then must be asked, how, and why does a good God allow evil to exist in His creation? Another question that is similar to these is where is God when such horrific acts of evil take place like the Holocaust or mass murders by religious zealots? God has given us the answer in His word from the very beginning. From Genesis 1, 2, and 3, I will show how these chapters explain why evil exists in a universe created by a good God.

It is important for you to understand that the events described in these three chapters are literal historical events. They are not mythological or allegorical. They are stated as a historical record. The actual Hebrew language they are stated in is not poetic but historical narrative. This is important because it takes these events out of the realm of the mystical and places them into reality. This makes the concepts of good and evil genuine parts of our existence rather than mere illusions. Good is real and evil is real. In the next chapter you will see how creation started out to be "very good."

ESTABLISHMENT OF GOOD

In the three synoptic gospels, Matthew, Mark, and Luke, Jesus is approached by a rich leader of the Jews with the question, "Good teacher what must I do to inherit eternal life?" Jesus responds with a question and a statement about good. His question was, "Why do you call me good?" The statement about good was, "No one is good except God alone." He makes two points. His first point is that the only true good that exists is God Himself. Second, if Jesus is good, He has to be God, something Jesus did not deny. The fact of the goodness of God is established in Genesis 1.

Genesis 1:1, "In the beginning God created the heavens and the earth." establishes the fact of God's pre-existence to the creation. In verse 3 of Genesis 1 God declares, "Let there be light!" Then in verse 4 it goes on to state, "And God saw that the light was good." I remember reading that statement and asking the question, "What or who is the source of this light and why is it good?" I knew that light is a form of energy and all energy requires a source. It is not self initiated. So, there has to be a source and the source had to be good.

The scriptures are a progressive revelation. What I mean by that is that as you read further in God's word more and more is revealed about God and His involvement in His creation. Reading further into God's word I was reminded of 1 John 1:5 that says, "...God is light, and in Him is no darkness at all." I also turned to James 1:17 that says, "God...is the Father of lights, and in Him is no shadow of turning." The apostle John reminded me that God Himself will be the source of light in the new heaven and new earth where he states in Revelation 22:5, "...the Lord God shall illumine them..." In the new heaven and new earth there will no longer be a need for the sun or the moon because God Himself will be the light needed then. Think about it. This is no different than what you find in the first three days of creation when God provided the needed light Himself until He created the sun, moon, and stars on the fourth day. So then, the light on day one was good because it was the light of God. The light was good because God is good and He was the source of that light.

In the Genesis 1 chapter, the word "good" is declared seven times. Except for the verse 3 "good," each of the other six are stated at the end of a given stage of creative activity with the same formula, "...and God saw that it was good." This declaration suggests to us that God was following a plan with six different stages and each stage, when completed, was a perfect expression of His goodness. God intended for His creation to be a perfect expression of Himself and His goodness. This is why Paul wrote in Romans 1:20, "For since the creation of the world His invisible attributes, His eternal power and divine nature, have been clearly seen, being understood through what has been made..." The whole of creation is an expression of God's goodness. Even in its fallen state you can still see His goodness in His creation's beauty and wonder all around you. You can also feel His emotions of love and compassion in you for those who are special to you.

What this all means is that before the fall of Adam and Eve into sin, the creation was totally good. Evil did not exist until they ate of the tree of knowledge of good and evil. In that original creation there was plenty of food; the water was pure; there was no pain and suffering, and death did not exist. Man was made in the image of God and all was "very good."

We know there was no death because all the living creatures including man only ate food from the vegetation God made. The vegetation was created with the ability to reproduce according to its own kind, but did not posses life like those in the animal kingdom created on the fifth and sixth day, and man created after the animals. Plants do not die in the same way animals and men do because they do not possess the Hebrew "nephesh" that is translated "life or soul." That is because God is the God of life, and death is not good because it has no part in the existence of the living God.

The original creation was totally good, a perfect expression of its Creator. Evil did not exist from the beginning. It was not a part of God's original finished creative work. This was foundational for me to understand if I was going to answer the question of how evil can exist in a creation created by a good God.

I learned as well that a totally good creation also established the foundation of the hope that all of us can have that God will finally do away with evil and establish a new creation where once again evil no longer exists. That is something we can look forward to if we accept God's provision that delivers us all from evil, His Son, the Lord Jesus Christ.

ESTABLISHMENT OF CHOICE

In order for God's creation to be totally good it had to include freedom. We have learned from history that life is not good under tyranny. In order for freedom to exist there has to be choice. We are free in America because we can choose our leaders, choose our way of faith, choose where we want to live, and the list goes on. Many people in the world do not have that kind of freedom. In Genesis 2 God establishes choice for Adam and Eve when He planted the Garden of Eden and placed within the middle of it the tree of life and the tree of the knowledge of good and evil.

I want to make sure you have a proper understanding of how Genesis 2 fits in God's progressive revelation of the creation week. There are those who try to say that Genesis 2 is a separate creation account than what is recorded in Genesis 1. They argue that there are contradictions between the two chapters. There are two principles that need to guide you in interpreting God's word. First, God is not the author of confusion and He does not contradict Himself. Second, God's word is a progressive revelation that adds information and gives clarification to what has already been revealed.

With these two principles in mind, you need to see that Genesis 2 is a further explanation of the events that took place on the sixth day Genesis 1 account. Genesis 2 gives you further information on how God created Adam and Eve in Genesis 1. It also tells of a place God prepared for them to live in, as well as where it was located, and what man was to do as the keeper of the garden. When you look at these two chapters in this way, you will see there is no confusion or contradiction between them.

God establishes choice as a part of Adam and Eve's relationship with Him, and brings the animals He had made in the first part of the day for Adam to name so he could learn that he was not an animal and that his wife was to meet all his needs. Covenant marriage was also established by the end of the day. That is the proper way of understanding Genesis 2 in light of God's progressive revelation.

During the sixth day God created Adam, planted a garden for him and Eve to live in and cultivate, and then He gave Adam a command that established choice as a part of the man's stewardship of God's creation. We learned in Genesis 1 that God created Adam and Eve in His own image. They were the perfect expression of God in created form. In order for them to be perfect expressions of God in His creation they had to be given free moral agency. In order for that free moral agency to be genuine they had to be given choice to obey God or to disobey God, and also be held responsible for their choice by being held accountable if they chose wrong.

This choice was paramount as I said earlier to establish freedom. There is no freedom without choice. But then choice also establishes the need for trust and makes love genuine rather than robotic. When God gave Adam and Eve the choice between the tree of life or the tree of the knowledge of good and evil, He was saying, "I want you to trust Me so that out of that trust you can learn to love Me."

That was the kind of relationship God wanted to have with those who He created to be most like Himself.

So, Genesis 2 establishes the principle of choice that made man's free moral agency legitimate. In the next chapter I want you to see how evil became possible after Adam and Eve made a wrong choice through listening to the lies of the serpent. Goodness was lost and evil was all that remained.

ESTABLISHMENT OF EVIL

In Genesis 1 I introduced you to how God, out of His goodness, created a universe that was a perfect expression of His goodness. So much so that He declared it "very good." In Genesis 2 you learned that in order for the creation to be very good, God had to allow those made in His image as free moral agents to have the freedom of choice. In Genesis 3 I will give you the explanation as to why evil exists in a universe created by a good God.

In direct rejection of God's directive to not eat of the tree of knowledge of good and evil through the serpent's deceptive cunning, Adam and Eve did not heed God's warning, "...in the day you eat from it you shall surely die." Though they were deceived, they were without excuse for they had been warned and thus had to be held accountable for their choice.

I will not get into the dynamics of the temptation. My purpose is to expose the results of Adam and Eve's choice to reject God's warning. Suffice it to say that the ultimate temptation was the prospect of becoming their own god just as Satan desired in Isaiah 14:14, "I will ascend above the heights of the clouds, I will make myself like the Most High." Satan used this same temptation against Adam and Eve when he blatantly lied by stating in Genesis 3:4-5, "...you surely shall not die. For God knows that in the day you eat from it your eyes will be opened and you will be like God, knowing good and evil."

The basis of Adam and Eve's rejection of God's command began first with a suggestion that God could not be trusted because He was withholding something from them, namely becoming equal to God by knowing good and evil. Secondly, the possibility of becoming equal to God was a thought they had not entertained before and so they became intrigued. The intrigue was too great and so they rejected God's warning and made a quick decision on the spur of the moment to act on Satan's proposition. As God had warned, it was a fatal mistake.

It can be said that Satan's temptation was at least a half truth. They did become like God in knowing good and evil, but what Satan did not tell them was that they would know good and evil from the position of evil unlike God who knows good and evil from the position of good. They did not understand that evil is all that God is not and that good is all that God is. When Adam and Eve were created they were totally good, but that good came from God's presence in them. If you remove God's good, all that is left is evil.

The establishment of evil is declared in Genesis 3:7 immediately after Adam and Eve ate the forbidden fruit. The verse states, "Then the eyes of both of them were opened and they knew that they were naked..." This statement makes it clear that an obvious transition had taken place. All of a sudden they "knew" something they had not known before. They became aware of their physical nakedness, something they had not been aware of before. We have to ask the question, "What took place to cause this transition?"

To answer the question we have to go back to God's warning given in Genesis 2:17, "...for in the day that you eat from it you shall surely die." The warning declares that an immediate death would take place if they ate from the wrong tree. Adam and Eve did not die physically but they became aware of their nakedness suggesting another kind of death. What kind of death would that be?

In Genesis 2:7, God breathed into Adam the breath or Spirit of God's own life. At the end of the chapter you saw that Adam and Eve did not know they were naked. Why was this so? Having been created in the image of God they were spiritual, God-breathed souls living in a physical body. That is why I believe Psalm 8:5 is rightly translated by the New American Standard as, "Thou has made him a little lower than God" rather than the angels. Man did not become lower than the angels until he fell into sin. Hebrews 1:14 tells us the angels were created to be ministering spirits for God in behalf of man. So Adam and Eve were alive spiritually as well as physically. The fact that they did not die physically on the day they ate of the tree of knowledge of good and evil tells you that they did die spiritually. In other words, God's presence of good was removed.

Since that time all the descendents of Adam and Eve, including you and me, have been born physically alive but spiritually dead. That is why Jesus told Nicodemus in John 3:7 "... you must be born again." This is not a second physical birth Jesus is referring to, but a rebirth of the spirit that is dead because of our sin. That spiritual death took place with Adam and Eve and has been passed down to each new generation of mankind.

Adam and Eve having died spiritually all of a sudden became physically focused, no longer good, and spiritually separated from God. Because of their fall into evil, they began to feel the shame of their nakedness and tried to cover themselves while on the other hand they began to feel fear of God and tried to hide from Him. Adam then, when confronted by God, expressed his fallen self centeredness by blaming Eve for giving him the fruit and blaming God for giving him Eve by saying in Genesis 3:12,"...The woman Thou gavest to be with me, she gave me from the tree, and I ate." Adam and Eve were no longer good. Why was this so?

The answer lies in the temptation they chose to act on. They were told by Satan through the serpent that if they ate of the forbidden tree they could become "like God, knowing good and evil." They in essence chose to reject

God's warning in order to become like God or even worse, equal to God. In doing so, they could become their own god. This rejection of God required a just response from God who honored Adam and Eve's God-given free moral agency. God's response then became, "if you want to be your own god, then you will be your own god for I will remove My presence from you." By God removing His presence from Adam and Eve they died spiritually and without the presence of God's good they became evil because when you remove good evil is all that is left. As God warned, eating from the wrong tree, they truly learned the knowledge of good and evil by experience.

Not only did Adam and Eve become evil but all of creation became evil as well. The creation was created to be the habitation of man. God created everything and then gave dominion over it all to Adam and Eve. It was a perfect place for them to dwell in as they reflected the goodness of God. By rejecting God, not only did God remove His presence from Adam and Eve, He also removed it from the creation as a whole. This had to be done in order for the creation to be a perfect reflection of Adam and Eve in their fallen condition. Due to their bad choice, evil became the order of the day in every aspect of the creation. That is why Romans 8:20 reads,

"For the creation was subjected to futility..." Evil is futile because separation from God is futile. Life and existence only has meaning when rooted and grounded in God and His goodness.

WHAT IS EVIL?

I have already hinted at the answer to the question, what is evil? You saw in Genesis 1:1 that God created everything in the universe, including the earth and man. He created it all very good meaning evil could not have any part in His finished work. You have to conclude then that evil was not created but is a consequence of Adam and Eve's rejection of God, not something that God included in His original creation.

So then what is evil? I said in the last chapter that when Adam and Eve chose to be their own god, God removed His presence from them. In doing so, Adam and Eve did not die physically but they did die spiritually.

Being left to themselves, they became evil as a consequence of God removing His presence from them. This being true, we can then conclude that evil is the absence of the presence of God's good. Without the presence of God's goodness, evil is all that is left. This is compatible with what Jesus said when He declared that only God is good. If only God is good then nothing can be good without the presence of His goodness.

I need to give clarification here. Even though God removed His goodness, He continued to maintain His creation as its source of energy and sovereign authority. This removal of His presence was apparently the withdrawal of the Holy Spirit's permeation of all that had been made. You can see the reversal of this in the return of the Holy Spirit on the day of Pentecost according to Jesus' promise in John 14:17, "...He abides with you, and will be in you."

Evil being the absence of God's good is a concept compatible with other phenomena we all observe. For example cold is the absence of heat. The way we measure cold is on the basis of how much heat is actually present. When an object that is cold is touched by a hot object the cold is not transferred to the hot object, the heat in the hot object is transferred to the cold object. Cold is a consequence of the removal of heat.

Another example is darkness. Darkness is the absence of light. When all light is removed, darkness does not increase in darkness, it is just dark. If you have a lighted bedroom and you open the door to your closet, darkness does not move out of the closet into the bedroom. The light in the bedroom moves into the closet to dispel the darkness in the closet. Darkness is a consequence of the removal of light.

One final example is death. Death is the absence of life. Once something dies it becomes dead. It cannot become anymore dead because dead is just dead. The Bible gives a description of this reality in Genesis 35:18 where the death of Rachel was described as she gave birth to Benjamin by saying, "And it came about as her soul was departing (for she died)..." Death was not entering her body. Her life was leaving her body. Death is the consequence of life leaving the body.

These three examples help you to comprehend how evil can be explained as being the absence of God's good. Evil was not created, instead it was all that was left when God's goodness was gone. That is why the Bible says, "There is none righteous, no not one." The fall was the establishment of the total depravity of man. That is why Paul could say in Romans 3:23, "For all have sinned and fall short of the glory of God." We have all sinned because, as descendents of Adam we posses his fallen nature that was passed on to us from him. We are all evil because, like Adam and Eve, the goodness of God is not in us.

WHAT IS GOOD?

Jesus has already told you what good is. Only God is good. The problem is in our fallen, depraved state of being we do not comprehend what that means. Our understanding is that God is perfect in His goodness as an infinite being. He is a God of sinless perfection. We seem to get that fairly well. Where we miss the mark in our comprehension about good is the idea that although we are not perfectly good like God, we can still obtain a certain level of goodness.

Here is the problem. Because there is no good in us we do not have the capacity to produce the only good that God accepts, His good. I run into this idea at times when witnessing to people about their need to be saved from their sins. Some people will reply, "Well I'm a good person, I don't steal, or I haven't murdered anybody. I pay my taxes and try to do what is right most of the time." This is a false understanding of our human condition that is not good in our evil state of being.

What we fail to realize is that in our fallen state we are evil to the core of our being. That is why Paul writes in Romans 3:10, quoting from Psalm 14:1-3 and Psalm 53:13, "There is none righteous, no not one." The Bible also says that even our goodness is like "filthy rags" (KJV) compared to God's goodness. Isaiah 64:6 in the New American Standard says it like this, "For all of us has become like one who is unclean. And all our righteous deeds are like a filthy garment."

In other words, no matter what we do, regardless of how good it might look to be in the eyes of mankind, our deeds are tainted by our sinful nature. Whether there is pride or self righteousness, wanting to be seen as a good person, or hoping to get something in return, God knows our hearts and sees our motives that will always be tainted by our fallen nature. Some examples would be Jesus telling us not to be like the hypocrites who pray out loud in the streets to be seen by men.

He said not to bring attention to ourselves when we fast, or give alms to the poor like so many do to gain the attention of men. We all have these fallen tendencies even when we try to do good because we are evil to the core of our being.

Because of this evil nature that is not able to produce any good that is acceptable to God, there is nothing we can do to make ourselves acceptable to God. That is why Christianity must be seen as the only true way to God. No other religion provides a way for doing away with our evil nature that stands in the way of God's acceptance of us. Without this acceptance we can never be allowed into God's presence. Without His goodness being restored in us as who we are in the same way Adam and Eve were before their rejection of God's warning of judgment, we must spend eternity separated from God. It is only those who reject Adam and Eve's original choice to become equal to God and humble themselves to submit to God's lordship who can then become part of His kingdom once again.

Those who continue to reject God as sovereign Lord over their lives continue to choose to be their own lord. As free moral agents, God can only accomplish in our lives what we are willing to let Him accomplish. He has given us the freedom to make our own choices and so He allows us to do so, even if it is a decision that goes against His will. If we want to do our own thing, God stands back and lets us do our own thing.

People ask where was God when Eve ate of the forbidden fruit and gave it to Adam as well? Why didn't God intervene? The answer is if God has given us the freedom of choice He has to let us make our choices, even when they are wrong. But not only does He allow us to make our choices, because He is the final authority in all things He must hold us accountable for our bad choices. He would not be good if He did not do so. Why? Because justice is a part of God's goodness and as a Holy God He must judge us when we violate His moral standards He incorporated into His creation as a perfect expression of Himself. God has to punish sin because sin violates His very being.

God's justice can be seen down through history. This justice is declared about God in Hebrews 10:30-31 where it says, "For we know Him (God) who said, 'Vengeance is Mine, I will repay.' And again, 'The Lord will judge His people.' It is a terrifying thing to fall into the hands of the living God." When the world became so vile it was beyond redeeming, God sent the flood. The same was true of Sodom and Gomorrah. Their evil had become so great that God finally destroyed them with fire. All the nations of history that declined into total depravity have been judged by God whether they be the nations of Canaan, the Egyptians, Assyrians, Babylonians, Israel, Persia, Greece, Rome, all the way down to today such as Hitler's Germany. It could become true of America if we do not mend our ways. Either now or in the final future judgment, God will bring His justice to right the wrong of all the evil done in His creation. We can depend on that.

Yes, God is holy and must punish sin. Sadly, all of us as members of the Adamic human race are sinners as Paul wrote in Romans 3:23, "For all have sinned and fall short of the glory of God." What is even worse, we have no goodness within ourselves to make us acceptable to God. Because of our evil nature, we have no means by which to make ourselves acceptable to God. We are not good in any way shape or form. Only God is good and only God is in the position of goodness to make us good again.

GOD'S ANSWER TO EVIL

God's only answer to evil is Himself. Only God is good and so only God can make us good in a way that is acceptable to Him. Because God is good, He is love, merciful, gracious, forgiving, patient, and kind. Consider the fruit of the Holy Spirit listed in Galatians 5:22-23, "...love, joy, peace, patience, kindness, goodness, faithfulness, gentleness, self-control,..." These attributes of His goodness gave Him the willingness to provide a way for all of us to become good again. That way back to becoming good again is Jesus, God's Son and Messiah. That is why Jesus said in John 14:6, "...I am the way, the truth, and the life, and no man comes to the Father except through me." Because we can do nothing to become good again, God did what needed to be done for us through Jesus. God's answer to evil is Himself in the person, Jesus Christ.

From the very beginning after the fall, God made a way for those who wanted to be restored to acceptance by God, even in their fallen condition. That way was through the shedding of blood. At the end of Genesis 3 you can see where God Himself killed animals, shedding their blood, in order to cover Adam and Eve's nakedness with the animal's skins. In chapter 4 you then see Cain and Abel bringing offerings to God. The only offering that was accepted by God was the sacrifice of sheep and their shed blood offered by Abel.

Apparently it was Abel who understood that the shedding of blood was God's provision for atoning for sin. This is made clear in Leviticus 17:11, "For the life of the flesh is in the blood, and I have given it to you on the alter to make atonement for your souls; for it is the blood by reason of the life that makes the atonement." Atonement means "covering." Covering of what? Covering for our sins. Hebrews 9:22 affirms this by stating, "...without the shedding of blood there is no forgiveness." So, God's provision to be restored to relationship with Him is the shedding of blood.

This shedding of blood covers our sins that are the result of our evil nature.

In God's progressive revelation, by the time of the New Testament and the coming of Jesus, it becomes clear that the sacrificial system of the Old Testament was a prophetic preparation for the one true shedding of blood. That prophetic system would be fulfilled through the shedding of Jesus' blood on the cross. His blood would atone for all sin of mankind once and for all. Hebrews 9:12 makes this point, "...and not through the blood of goats and calves, but through His own blood, He entered the holy place (in heaven before the Father) once for all, having obtained eternal redemption." It is through the blood of Jesus that we are redeemed back to God in restored relationship in His goodness.

There are certain things about Jesus that had to be true in order for Him to have the power to make us good again through His sacrifice on our behalf. He had to be God to be good. He had to be a man to do for mankind what we cannot do for ourselves because of our evil state. He had to be without sin. Unlike Adam and Eve, He had to be totally obedient to the Father. Let's look at each of these attributes of Jesus.

First, Jesus had to be God to be good. To be the perfect sacrifice, Jesus had to be good just as Adam and Eve were before their being deceived by Satan. Jesus had to succeed where Adam and Eve failed in order to become the new descendent of those who were to be made good again. He had to do so from a position of goodness to overcome the consequence of evil brought on by Adam and Eve. In order to be good, He had to be God because only God is good.

The Old Testament prophesied the Messiah would be God. Isaiah 7:14 states that He would be called, "God with us." Isaiah 9:6 declares, "He will be called...mighty God, eternal Father..." Jesus claimed to be God. He made statements like, "If you have seen Me you have seen the Father." "I and the Father are one (the same)." Before Abraham was I Am."

The disciples said Jesus was God. John 1:1 states, "In the beginning was the Word, and the Word was with God, and the Word was God." Peter wrote of Jesus in 2 Peter 1:1, "...by the righteousness of our God and Savior, Jesus Christ." Thomas declared when he saw the resurrected Jesus, "My Lord and my God." Paul wrote of Jesus in Colossians 1:17 when he said, "And He is before all things, and in Him all things hold together." The Bible makes it clear that Jesus is God in a physical, human body. Jesus being God means He was totally good.

Jesus had to be a man. It was Adam and Eve who sinned against God. In doing so, they became evil having been left to themselves by the removal of the presence of God's goodness. Since then their fallen condition has been passed down through all of their descendents so that the whole human race is fallen in sin. Just as evil came through one man, evil could only be eradicated by a man. The blood of bulls, goats, sheep, and or doves could only be symbolic. Their blood did not have the life of man in it. It is the life in the blood that makes atonement for sin. Only the life of a man could atone for the sins of man. Paul makes this point in Roman's 5:19, "For as through the one man's disobedience, the many were made sinners, even so through the obedience of the One (man) the many will be made righteous."

So then, how could Jesus be God and man at the same time? The answer is found in the virgin birth. Through the seed of His human mother, Mary, Jesus descended from Adam. But, He was a new creation in that the Holy Spirit created the necessary chromosome that allowed Jesus to have a human body without having the fallen nature of Adam passed to Him. Hebrews 10:5 makes this point by saying, "Therefore, when He (The Messiah) comes into the world, He says, 'Sacrifice and offering Though hast not desired, but a body Thou hast prepared for me.' " Apparently, the fallen nature is passed on through the man and the woman, not the woman alone, so Jesus could be descended from Adam through Mary without his evil nature. This was prophesied by God in Genesis 3:15 where He said the "seed" of the woman would crush the head of the seed of the serpent. Jesus is fully God and fully man.

Jesus, having to be a man with the blood of Adam running through His veins is consistent with the concept of the "kinsman redeemer" in the Old Testament. In the story of Ruth, Boaz was second in line as Ruth's kinsman redeemer. Because he was the second closest blood relative of Ruth's dead husband he could marry her after the closest blood relative refused to carry on the heritage of his dead cousin. Jesus, in order to be our kinsman redeemer, had to be a blood relative. Adam, Eve, and their heritage having died spiritually because of their sin could only be redeemed by their closest blood relative who was without sin, Jesus Christ our kinsman redeemer.

Jesus had to be without sin. You can see that was made possible by the virgin birth as well. The impact of Adam's original sin was not passed on to Jesus through a human father. He had a human body through Mary but not the fallen nature of Adam.

Why is this so very important? The Bible tells us that the wages of sin is death. If Jesus had a sin nature like Adam, He like all the rest of us, would have had to die for his own sin problem. But because He was without sin or a fallen nature, death had no claim on Him and so He was free to die for our sins and not His own.

Jesus being sinless without the evil nature of Adam in his fallen state was the perfect sacrifice to undo what Adam and Eve had done to make it possible for evil to exist in God's good creation. But one thing remains that had to be true about Jesus. Unlike Adam and Eve, He had to be totally obedient to the Father's will.

Having a free will, Adam and Eve had to be tested to determine their trust in God and their willingness to be faithful to Him to establish a genuine love relationship. They failed the test. Jesus' first recorded act of obedience was His baptism where He expressed His surrender to His Father's will for Him to die in behalf of man's sin.

The Father responded with, "This is my beloved Son in whom I am well pleased." What was it that pleased the Father? It was His obedience.

He then went into the wilderness and was tempted by Satan for forty days. Actually, His temptation was far more severe than what Adam and Eve experienced. Did Jesus have the ability to fail His temptation test as Adam and Eve did? Yes He did. He had free will just as they did, but His trust of His Father, love for His Father, and commitment to His Father's will was far greater than the temptation to do His own will.

You can also see His obedience expressed in the fact that He never said or did anything unless it was His Father's will. He was always getting alone to pray to seek the Father's direction for Him. Jesus stated this in John 5:30, "...because I do not seek My own will but the will of Him who sent Me." The great example of this was His prayer in the garden when facing death on the cross. He prayed, "...nevertheless not My will but Thy will be done." Jesus was obedient to His Father from the beginning to the end of His life here on earth.

Jesus, being good, without sin, the Son of God and the Son of Man, and in total obedience to His Father is God's answer to evil. As the second Adam, He has won the victory over sin and death through His death and resurrection. He regained the position of dominion over creation lost by Adam and Eve to Satan. He shed His blood on the cross to pay the penalty for sin, and rose again to establish new life to all those who believe in Him. All who believe in Him become good again with the goodness of the presence of God. How does that happen?

When you put your faith in Jesus' finished work on the cross, confess your sins, and invite Him into your heart as an act of your will, God takes the righteousness or goodness of Jesus and applies it to you. Just as the fallen nature of Adam was passed on to you by birth, the righteousness of Jesus is passed on to you by faith resulting in the new birth. At the moment of salvation, the new birth, the Holy Spirit comes to dwell in you restoring the goodness of God in you by His presence.

You must remember though, that it is God's goodness in you that comes from Him and not from you. As a Christian, you become involved in a battle between your old evil nature and your new nature until you die or Jesus comes again to restore His goodness to His creation. This was Paul's experience when He cried out as a born again Christian dealing with his fallen nature in Roman's 7:24-25, "Wretched man that I am, who will deliver me from this body of death? Thanks be to God through Jesus Christ our Lord." It is through Jesus and His Holy Spirit that He overcomes evil in us. He does so by your obedience to Jesus rather than doing the will of your evil nature that no longer reigns over you. We all overcome our evil with the goodness of Jesus by the presence of His Holy Spirit who is the expression of God's goodness restored in us.

After you become a Christian, you have the Holy Spirit living in you. But, you still have to deal with your fallen nature. In 1 Corinthians 2 and 3 Paul explains that there are three kinds of people: Natural Man, Fleshly Christians, and Spiritual Christians. The natural man describes all those who have never experienced the new birth. The Holy Spirit and His goodness is not in them. The fleshly Christian has the Holy Spirit dwelling in him but he has not given Him full control of His life. The spiritual Christian seeks to give the Holy Spirit full control of his life.

The fleshly Christian serves God in his own natural human abilities. The spiritual Christian allows the Holy Spirit to do His work through him. The service of the fleshly Christian is not acceptable to God because it is not good coming from the Christian's fallen nature. The service of the spiritual Christian is accepted by God because it is produced by the Holy Spirit's good.

Paul describes the difference in 1 Corinthians 3:12-13, "Now if any man builds upon the foundation (Jesus Christ Himself) with gold, silver, precious stones, wood, hay, straw, each man's work will become evident; for the day (judgment) will show it, because it is to be revealed by fire; and the fire itself will test the quality of each man's work (fleshly or spiritual). If any man's work which he has built upon it (the foundation of Jesus Christ) remains, he shall receive a reward." Spiritual service is the gold, silver, precious stones which are refined by fire and will remain. The human nature fleshly service is the wood, hay, and straw, which will be burned up. Even as a Christian, you have no good in yourself that can be acceptable to God. Only His good produced by the Holy Spirit through you pleases Him.

When you put your faith and trust in Jesus, your future in heaven is secure in Him. But, you still have a life to live after becoming a Christian. You can use that life to bring God's goodness to those around you by allowing the Holy Spirit to have complete control of your life.

When Jesus taught us all to pray in Matthew 6:10, He told us to say to the Father, "...Thy kingdom come, Thy will be done on earth as it is in heaven..." The way God brings His kingdom to earth is by expressing His goodness through you. He does this as you are led by the Holy Spirit to say and do the Father's will each day living for Him and not yourself just as Jesus did during His ministry here on earth. What God wants to do is overcome the evil of this world with His good through you.

CONCLUSION

God's answer to evil in His creation is His only begotten Son, Jesus Christ. Good is restored in all of those who put their faith and trust in Him and His goodness rather than their own. But then you might say, Jesus came 2,000 years ago and there is still evil in the world. Yes that is true, but look at all the good that has come since then. The impact of Christianity is seen throughout the world in changed lives, orphanages, hospitals, schools, non-profit ministries of all kinds working to overcome pain and suffering. The Christian worldview still influences society for good in upholding the sanctity of life, the dignity of the individual, and the concepts of freedom and equality.

Yes, a lot of hurt, pain, and suffering still happen in the world, but God is not finished yet. All through history nations have risen to power for a period of time only to be replaced by another when those nations became so contemptible because of their evil practices. God's justice has been shown in the rise and fall of these nations, but that justice will be finally brought to bear on evil once and for all when Jesus comes again and establishes His 1,000 year rule on earth (Revelation 20:6) and then has the final judgment where all evil will be vanquished in the lake of fire as seen in Revelation 20:15, "And if anyone's name was not found written in the book of life, he was thrown into the lake of fire." No one gets away with anything in the end.

Only those who have received God's forgiveness through the shed blood of Jesus Christ will be spared according to God's promise in Romans 10:13, "Whosoever shall call upon the name of the Lord shall be saved."

In the last two chapters of The Revelation of Jesus Christ, we see that good will be totally restored and evil will be totally overcome by the presence of God. Revelation 21:3-4 proclaims, "And I heard a loud voice from the throne saying, 'Behold, the tabernacle of God is among men, and He shall dwell among them, and they shall be His peoples, and God Himself shall be among them, and He shall wipe away every tear from their eyes, and there shall no longer be any death; there shall no longer be any mourning, or crying, or pain: the first things have passed away.' "

In the new heaven and earth, God's goodness will permeate every aspect of their existence because of God's presence, and all the suffering caused by evil will be eradicated. The wonder of God's original good creation that was declared by God to be "very good" will be even more glorious than the first. Evil will never to be possible again.

Are you one of those who have given up on God because you have been disillusioned by the effects of evil in the world? Let me tell you that God is not the problem He is the solution in the person of Jesus Christ. I encourage you to put your faith and trust in Jesus and He will heal your soul while giving you hope beyond any of the evil that has impacted your life. You can overcome evil with the goodness of Jesus controlling your life by the presence and power of His Holy Spirit. Pray to Jesus right now and let Him restore His goodness in you as He forgives all your sins and begins to make you into a new person.

Overcome Evil With Good

by Steve Kern

Oh God, overcome evil with good in me by Thee

Oh God, when my evil eyes see the faults of others

Give me Your eyes to see my faults first

Oh God, when my evil ears hear the curse of others

Give me Your ears to hear the souls that thirst

Oh God, when my evil hands withhold their
help for others

Give me Your hands that open wide to feed

Oh God, when my evil feet would walk
away from others

Give me Your feet that run to every need

Oh God, when my evil heart holds contempt
for others

Give me Your heart that loves even the lowest one

And God, when my evil self says me instead of others

Give me Your Self that died to self and won

Oh God, overcome evil with good in me by Thee

SOURCES

Geisler, Norman L., Turek, Frank, 2004, I Don't Have Enough Faith to Be an Atheist, Crossway Books, Wheaton, Illinois.

Kern, Steve, 2007, No Other God's, Kern Enterprises, Oklahoma City, Oklahoma.

Lyle, Jason, 2009, The Ultimate Proof of Creation, Master Books, Green Forest, Arkansas.

Morris, Henry M., 1976, The Genesis Record, Baker Book House, Grand Rapids, Michigan.

Morris, Henry M., 1989, The Long War Against God, Baker Book House, Grand Rapids, Michigan.

www.ingramcontent.com/pod-product-compliance
Lightning Source LLC
Chambersburg PA
CBHW060041040426
42331CB00032B/1997